I0481636

Copyright

All rights reserved. No part of this publication may be reproduced, distributed, or transmitted in any form or by any means, including photocopying, recording, or other electronic or mechanical methods, without the prior written permission of the publisher, except in the case of brief quotations embodied in critical reviews and certain other non-commercial uses permitted by copyright law.

Get This As a FREE Audiobook via Amazon's Audible.com

Visit: Bookskim.com/free

Introduction

For the last couple of years, Google Adsense has dominated forums, discussions and newsletters all over the Internet. Already, there are tales of fabulous riches to be made and millions made by those who are just working from home. It seems that Google Adsense have already dominated the internet marketing business and is now considered the easiest way to making money online.

The key to success with Adsense is the placing of ads on pages that are receiving high traffic for high demand keywords. The higher the cost-per-click to the advertiser, the more you will receive per click from your site. Obviously, it does not pay to target low cost-per-click keywords and place them on pages that do not receive hits.

With all the people getting online and clicking away everyday, it is no wonder why Google Adsense has become an instant hit.

For some who are just new to this market, it would be a blow to their pride knowing that their homepage is buried somewhere in the little ads promoting other people's services. But then, when they get the idea that they are actually earning more money that way, all doubts and skepticism is laid to rest.

There are two major, and clever, factors that some successful webmaster and publishers are learning to blend together in order to make money easier using Adsense.

1. Targeting high traffic pages on your website. If you check on your logs, you will discover that many of your visitors are taking advantage of the free affiliate marketing resources and ebooks that you are offering on your site. In simple words, your ads are working effectively and are generating more clicks. It also means more money for you.
2. Placing Adsense links on pages that are producing little, or better yet, no profit. By placing Adsense on a free resources page, you will reduce the amount of potential customers being lost to other sites. Tricky, but effective nonetheless.

When learned to work effectively, these two factors are actually a good source of producing a minimal amount of revenue from a high traffic page. Many people are using this strategy to pick up some extra and cash with Adsense. This is also especially rewarding to informational sites that focus their efforts on delivering powerful affiliate link free content to their visitors. Now they can gain a monetary return on their services.

With the many techniques that people are now learning on how to make the easiest money by their Adsense, it is not surprising that Google is trying everything to update and polish their Adsense in order to maintain their good image.

The possibility of adding is 2nd tier in Adsense is not impossible. With all the people spending more time in their Adsense now and still more getting into this line of marketing, there is no doubt about the many new improvements yet to be made. Imagine the smiles on the faces of the webmasters and publishers all around the world if ever they sign up for sub-affiliates and double or even triple the amount that they are already earning.

The one particularly handy money-making feature that is available with Adsense now is the ability to filter out up to 200 urls. These gives webmasters the option to block out low value offers from their pages as well as competitors to their websites. Talk about taking only those that are advantageous and discarding the ones that seem "useless".

With Google Adsense, the possibilities are limitless. Yet there is also the possibility of someone taking advantage of the easy money process that this internet marketing is doing.

If you think more about it, these negative factors may force Google to break down and thrash Adsense in the process.

If that happens, people would have to go back to the old ways of internet marketing that does not make money online as easy as Adsense.

For now, however, Google Adsense is here to stay. As long as there are people wanting to earn some easy cash online just using their talents, the future ahead is looking good. Besides with all the strict guidelines that Google is enforcing over Adsense, it will take awhile for the Adsense privileges to be spammed and even terminated.

3 Reasons Why Adsense Is Essential For Content Sites

To know why Adsense is essential for your content sites is to know first how this works.

The concept is really simple, if you think about it. The publisher or the webmaster inserts a java script into a certain website. Each time the page is accessed, the java script will pull advertisements from the Adsense program.

The ads that are targeted should therefore be related to the content that is contained on the web page serving the ad. If a visitor clicks on an advertisement, the webmaster serving the ad earns a portion of the money that the advertiser is paying the search engine for the click.

The search engine is the one handling all the tracking and payments, providing an easy way for webmasters to display content-sensitive and targeted ads without having the hassle to solicit advertisers, collect funds, monitor the clicks and statistics which could be a time-consuming task in itself.

It seems that there is never a shortage of advertisers in the program from which the search engine pulls the Adsense ads. Also webmasters are less concerned by the lack of information search engines are providing and are more focused in making cash from these search engines.

The first reason why Adsense is essential for content sites is because it already has come a long way in understanding the needs of publishers and webmasters.

Together with its continuous progression is the appearance of more advanced system that allows full ad customization. Webmasters are given the chance to choose from many different types of text ad formats to better complement their website and fit their webpage layout.

The different formatting enables the site owners the possibility of more click through from visitors who may or may not be aware of what they are clicking on. It can also appeal to the people visiting thus make them take that next step of looking up what it is all about. This way the people behind the Adsense will get their content read and making profit in the process.

The second reason is the ability of the Adsense publishers to track not only how their sites are progressing but also the earnings based on the webmaster-defined channels. The recent improvements in the search engines gives webmasters the capability to monitor how their ads are performing using customizable reports that has the capacity to detail page impressions, clicks and click-through rates.

Webmasters and publishers can now track specific ad formats, colors and pages within a website. Trends are also easily spotted.

With the real-time reporting at hand, the effectiveness of the changes made will be assessed quickly. There would be time to sort out the contents that people are making the most clicks on. The ever-changing demands would be met while generating cash for the webmasters and publishers.

The more flexible tools are also allowing webmasters to group web pages by URL, domain, ad type or category, which will provide them some accurate insight on which pages, ads and domains are performing best.

The last and final reason is that the advertisers have realized the benefits associated having their ads served on targeted websites. Thus increasing the possibility that a prospective web surfer will have an interest in their product and services. All because of the content and its constant maintenance.

As opposed to those who are no using Adsense in their sites, they are given the option of having other people do their content for them, giving them the benefit of having successful and money-generating web sites.

Adsense is all about targeted content, the more targeted your content is, the more target the search engines' ads will be. There are some web masters and publishers who are focused more on their site contents and how best to maintain them rather than the cash that the ads will generate for them. This is the part where the effectiveness is working its best.

There was a time when people were not yet aware of the money to be achieved from advertisements. The cash generated only came into existence when the webmasters and publishers realized how they can make Adsense be that generator. In those days, the content were the most important factors that is taken quite seriously. It still is. With the allure of money, of course.

The Basics On How TO Start Making Money With Adsense

Adsense is considered as one of the most powerful tool in a website publisher's arsenal. It enables a person to monetize their sites easily. If used properly, it can generate a very large and healthy income for them. However if you are not using them rightly and just maximizing the income you squeeze from it, you are actually leaving a lot of money on the table. Something all people hate doing.

How you can start earning money with Adsense can be done easily and quickly. You will be amazed at the results you will be getting in such a short period of time.

Start by writing some quality content articles which are also keyword incorporated. There are a lot of people given the gift of being good with words. Writing comes easy for them. Why not make it work in such a way that you will be earning some extra cash in the process.

There are actually three steps to put into mind before you begin writing your ads and having an effective Adsense.

Keyword search. Find some popular subjects, keywords or phrase. Select the ones which you think has more people clicking through. This is actually a keyword selector and suggestion tool that some sites are offering to those who are just their Adsense business.

Writing articles. Start writing original content with keywords from the topics that you have achieved in your search. Take note that search engines are taking pride in the quality of their articles and what you will be writing should keep up with their demands.

Quality content site. Build a quality content site incorporated with Adsense ads that is targeting the subject and keywords of your articles and websites. This is where all that you've done initially will go to and this is also where they will prove their worth to you.

The proper positioning of your ads should be done with care. Try to position your ads where surfers are most likely to click on them. According to research, the one place that surfers look first when they visit a certain site is the top left. The reason behind this is not known. Maybe it is because some of the most useful search engine results are at the top of all other rankings. So visitors tend to look in that same place when browsing through other sites.

Some of those who are just starting at this business may think they are doing pretty well already and thinking that their clickthrough rates and CPM figures are quite healthy. However, there are more techniques and styles to generate more clicks to double your earnings. By knowing these techniques and working them to your advantage, you will realize that you will be getting three times more than other people who have been previously doing what they are doing.

Finally, Adsense has some excellent tracking statistics that allows webmasters and publishers to track their results across a number of site on a site by site, page by page, or any other basis you wanted. You should be aware oft his capability and make the most of it because it is one powerful tool that will help you find out which ads are performing best. This way, you can fine tune your Adsense ads and focus more on the ones being visited the most rather than those who are being ignored.

Another thing you should know. Banners and skyscrapers are dead. Ask the experts. So better forget about banners and skyscrapers. Surfers universally ignore these kinds of ad formats. The reason behind this is that they are recognized as an advert and advert are rarely of any interest that's why people ignore them.

To really start making money with Adsense, you should have a definite focus on what you wanted to achieve and how you will go about achieving them. As with any other kind of business ventures, time is needed coupled with patience.

Do not just ignore your site and your Adsense once you have finished accomplishing them. Spare some time, even an hour, making adjustments to the Adsense ads on your sites to quickly trigger your Adsense income.

Give it a try and you would not regret having gotten into Adsense in the first place.

5 Ways To Improve Your Adsense Earnings

If webmasters want to monetize their websites, the great way to do it is through Adsense. There are lots of webmasters struggling hard to earn some good money a day through their sites. But then some of the "geniuses" of them are enjoying hundreds of dollars a day from Adsense ads on their websites. What makes these webmasters different from the other kind is that they are different and they think out of the box.

The ones who have been there and done it have quite some useful tips to help those who would want to venture into this field. Some of these tips have boosted quite a lot of earnings in the past and is continuously doing so.

Here are 5 proven ways on how best to improve your Adsense earnings.

1. Concentrating on one format of Adsense ad. The one format that worked well for

1. the majority is the Large Rectangle (336X280). This same format have the tendency to result in higher CTR, or the click-through rates. Why choose this format out of the many you can use? Basically because the ads will look like normal web links, and people, being used to clicking on them, click these types of links. They may or may not know they are clicking on your Adsense but as long as there are clicks, then it will all be for your advantage.

2. Create a custom palette for your ads. Choose a color that will go well with the background of your site. If your site has a white background, try to use white as the color of your ad border and background. The idea to patterning the colors is to make the Adsense look like it is part of the web pages. Again, This will result to more clicks from people visiting your site.

3. Remove the Adsense from the bottom pages of your site and put them at the top. Do not try to hide your Adsense. Put them in the place where people can see them quickly. You will be amazed how the difference between Adsense

1. locations can make when you see your earnings.
2. Maintain links to relevant websites. If you think some sites are better off than the others, put your ads there and try to maintaining and managing them. If there is already lots of Adsense put into that certain site, put yours on top of all of them. That way visitor will see your ads first upon browsing into that site.
3. Try to automate the insertion of your Adsense code into the webpages using SSI (or server side included). Ask your web administrator if your server supports SSI or not. How do you do it? Just save your Adsense code in a text file, save it as "adsense text", and upload it to the root directory of the web server. Then using SSI, call the code on other pages. This tip is a time saver especially for those who are using automatic page generators to generate pages on their website.

These are some of the tips that have worked well for some who want to generate hundreds and even thousands on their websites. It is important to know though that ads are displayed because it fits the interest of the people viewing them. So focusing on a specific topic should be your primary purpose because the displays will be especially targeted on a topic that persons will be viewing already.

Note also that there are many other Adsense sharing the same topic as you. It is best to think of making a good ad that will be somewhat different and unique than the ones already done. Every clickthrough that visitors make is a point for you so make every click count by making your Adsense something that people will definitely click on.

Tips given by those who have boosted their earnings are just guidelines they want to share with others. If they have somehow worked wonders to some, maybe it can work wonders for you too. Try them out into your ads and see the result it will bring.

If others have done it, there is nothing wrong trying it out for yourself.

Monetizing Your Website With Adsense

Many are now realizing that good money is made from this source of revenue. Try the simple mathematical computation of multiplying those clicks for every page on your website and you get a summation of earnings equivalent to a monthly residual income with that little effort you have made.

Google Adsense is a fast and easy way for website publishers of all sizes to display relevant and text-based Google ads on their website's content pages and earn money in the process.

The ads displayed are related to what your users are looking for on your site. This is the main reason why you both can monetize and enhance your content pages using Adsense.

How much you will be earning will depend on how much the advertisers are willing to pay. It will depend also on the keywords required. If the keywords the advertiser have chosen are in high demand, you could receive more dollars per click. On the other hand, low demand keywords will earn you just a few cents per click.

How can you start making profits out of your website using Adsense?

1. Sign up for an Adsense account. It will only take a few minutes of your time.
2. When the site is accepted, you will be receiving a clip code to include in your web pages. You can insert this code on as many pages or web sites that you want. The AdWords will start appearing immediately after.
3. You will be earning a few cents or some dollars per click when someone starts clicking on the AdWords displayed on any of your web pages. Trying to earn false revenues by repetitively clicking on your own ads is a no-no. This will result in a penalty or the possibility of your site being eliminated. The money you have already earned may be lost because of this.
4. View your statistics. Adsense earnings can be checked anytime by logging into your web site account.

Once you got your account working, you may still want to pattern them to the many sites that are earning more money than you are. It is important to note that there are factors affecting how your website will perform and the amount of money it will give you.

It is a common practice that when a site earning money, the tendency is for the owner to want to make more out of what they are getting already. It usually takes some time combined with trial and error to attain what you want for your Adsense contents.

Time and some important factors that you can practice and use.

How do you increase your Adsense earnings

1. Choose one topic per page. It is best to write a content for your page with just a few targeted phrases. The search engine will then serve ads that are more relevant which will then result in higher clickthoughs.
2. Using white space around your ad. This can make your ad stand out from the rest of your page so visitors can spot them easily. There are also other choices of colors you can use, provided by search engines, which can harmonize the color of your ad with the web page color.
3. Test your ad placement. It is recommended to use the vertical format

1. that runs down the side of the web page to get more positive results. You can also try both horizontal and vertical formats for a certain period of time to see which one will give you better results.
2. More content-based pages. Widen the theme of your website by creating pages that focus more on your keyword phrases. This will optimize the pages for the search engines. It can not only attract traffic but also make them more relevant for the AdWords to be displayed.
3. Site Build It. This is the perfect tool to be used for creating lots of Adsense revenues. Site Build It has all the tools necessary to quickly achieve a keyword-rich site that can rank high in the search engines. This will also produce a flow of traffic to your site of highly targeted visitors.

Most webmasters know that Adsense generates a sizeable source of additional advertising income. That is why most of them use it to go after high paying keywords. They have with them the lists that tells what the keywords are and have already used various methods of identifying them. And yet, after putting up these supposed-to-be high paying keywords into their pages, the money they expected to come rolling in is not really coming in.

What is it that they are doing wrong?

Having the pages is with the proper keywords is one thing. But driving visitors to those pages is another matter and often the factor that is lacking.

The thing is, to get visitors to your high paying keyword pages, you need to optimize your site navigation.

Stop for a moment and think about how visitors are using your website. After a visitor has landed on a certain page, they have the tendency to click on another page that sounds interesting. They get there because of the other links that appears on a page that they initially landed on. This is site navigation. It is all about enabling visitors to move about your site. And one way of maximizing your Adsense earnings.

A typical website have menu links on each page. The wording on these links is what grabs a visitor's attention and gets them to click on one of the links that will take them to another page of that website. Links that have "free' or "download" are oftentimes good attention-grabbers.

This navigation logic can also be applied to driving traffic to your high paying pages. There are some websites that are getting a lot of traffic from search engines, but have low earnings. The trick is to try and use come cleverly labeled links to get the visitors off that pages and navigate them to the higher earning ones. This is one great way of turning real cheap clicks to real dollars.

Before you begin testing if this same style will work for you and you website, you need to have two things. Something to track and compare and some high earning pages you want to funnel your site traffic to. An option is to select a few of your frequently visited pages. This is ensuring fast result to come by.

Now, the next thing to do is think of ways to get visitors viewing a particular page to try and click on the link that will take them to your high earning pages. Come up with a catchy description for that link. Come up with a catchy and unique description for the link. Think of something that people do not get to see everyday. That will trigger their curiosity enough to try and see what that was all about.

You can also use graphics to grab your readers' attention. There is no limitation to what you can do to make your link noticeable. If you are after the success of your site, you will do everything it takes just to achieve that goal. Just be creative. As far as many Adsense advertisers are concerned, there are no written and unwritten laws to follow regarding what they write. Just as long as you do not overstep the guidelines of the search engines, then go for it.

Also remember that it is all about location, location and location. Once the perfect attention grabbing description has been achieved, you have to identify the perfect spot on your page to position that descriptive link to your high paying page.

There is nothing wrong with visiting other websites to see how they are going about maximizing their site navigation. "Hot pages" or "Most read" lists are very common and overly used already. Get to know the ones that many websites are using and do not try to imitate them.

Another way of doing it is to try and use different texts on different pages. That way you will see the ones that work and what does not. Try to mix things around also. Put links on top and sometimes on the bottom too. This is how you go about testing which ones get more clicks and which ones are being ignored.

Let the testing begin. Testing and tracking until you find the site navigation style that works best for you site.

Using Other Peoples Info To Increase Your Adsense Cash

Adsense is really making a huge impact on the affiliate marketing industry nowadays. Because of this, weak affiliate merchants have the tendency to die faster than ever and ad networks will be going to lose their customers quickly.

If you are in a losing rather than winning in the affiliate program you are currently into, maybe it is about time to consider going into the Adsense marketing and start earning some real cash.

Google is readily providing well written and highly relevant ads that are closely chosen to match the content on your pages. You do not have to look for them yourselves as the search engine will be the doing the searching for you from other people's source.

You do not have to spend time in choosing different kind of ads for different pages. And no codes to mess around for different affiliate programs.

You will be able to concentrate on providing good and quality content, as the search engines will be the ones finding the best ads in which to put your pages on.

You are still allowed to add Adsense ads even if you already have affiliate links on your site. It is prohibited, however, to imitate the look and feel of the Google ads for your affiliate links.

You can filter up to 200 URLs. That gives you a chance to block ads for the sites that do not meet your guidelines. You can also block competitors. Though it is unavoidable that Adsense may be competing for some space on web sites that all other revenues are sharing.

Owners of small sites are allowed to plug a bit of a code into their sites and instantly have relevant text ads that appeal to your visitors appear instantly into your pages. If you own many sites, you only need to apply once. It makes up for having to apply to many affiliate programs.

The only way to know how much you are already earning is to try and see. If you want out, all you have to do is remove the code from your site.

The payment rates can vary extremely. The payment you will be receiving per click depends on how much advertisers are paying per click to advertise with the use of the AdWords. Advertisers can pay as little as 5 cents and as high as $10-12, sometimes even more than that too. You are earning a share of that money generated.

If your results remain stagnant, it can help if you try and build simple and uncluttered pages so that the ads can catch the visitor's eyes more. It sometimes pay to differ from the usual things that people are doing already. It is also a refreshing sight for your visitor once they see something different for a change.

Publishers also have the option of choosing to have their ads displayed only on a certain site or sites. It is also allowed to have them displayed on a large network of sites. The choice would be depending on what you think will work best for your advantage.

To get an idea if some Adsense ads you see on the search engines has your pages, try to find web pages that have similar material to the content you are planning to create and look up their Adsense ads.

It is important to note that you cannot choose certain topics only. If you do this, search engines will not place Adsense ads on your site and you will be missing out a great opportunity in making hundreds and even thousands of dollars cash.

It is still wise to look at other people's information and format your Adsense there. Just think about it as doing yourself a favor by not having to work too hard to know what content to have.

With all the information that people need in your hands already, all you have to do is turn them as your profits. It all boils down to a gain and gain situation both for the content site owners and the webmasters or publishers.

Make other people's matter your own and starting earning some extra cash

How To Avoid Getting Your Adsense Account Terminated

Google, being the undisputable leader in search engines from then until now, is placing a high importance on the quality and relevancy of its search engines.

Most especially now that the company is public property. In order to keep the shareholders and users of its engines happy, the quality of the returned results are given extreme importance.

For this same reason, doing the wrong things in the Adsense and other forms of advertisements, whether intentionally or unintentionally, will result in a severe penalty, may get you banned and even have your account terminated. Nothing like a good action taken to keep wrongdoers from doing the same things over again.

So for those who are thinking of getting a career in Adsense, do not just think of the strategies you will be using to generate more earnings. Consider some things first before you actually get involved.

Hidden texts. Filling your advertisement page with texts to small to read, has the same color as the background and using css for the sole purpose of loading them with rich keywords content and copy will earn you a penalty award that is given to those who are hiding links.

Page cloaking. There is a common practice of using browser or bot sniffers to serve the bots of a different page other than the page your visitors will see. Loading a page with a bot that a human user will never see is a definite no-

no. This is tricking them to click on something that you want but they may not want to go to.

Multiple submissions. Submitting multiple copies of your domain and pages is another thing to stay away from. For example, trying to submit a URL of an Adsense as two separate URL's is the same as inviting trouble and even termination.

Likewise, this is a reason to avoid auto submitters for those who are receiving submissions. Better check first if your domain is submitted already an a certain search engine before you try to submit to it again. If you see it there, then move on. No point contemplating whether to try and submit there again.

Link farms. Be wary of who and what are you linking your Adsense to. The search engines know that you cannot control your links in. But you can certainly control what you link to. Link farming has always been a rotten apple in the eyes of search engines, especially Google. That is reason enough to try and avoid them. Having a link higher than 100 on a single page will classify you as a link farm so try and not to make them higher than that.

Page rank for sale. If you have been online for quite some time, you will notice that there are some sites selling their PR links or trading them with other sites. If you are doing this, expect a ban anytime in the future. It is okay to sell ads or gain the link. But doing it on direct advertisement of your page rank is a way to get on search engines bad side.

Doorways. This is similar to cloaking pages. The common practice of a page loaded with choice keyword ads aimed at redirecting visitors to another "user-friendly" page is a big issue among search engines. There are many seo firms offering this kind of services. Now that you know what they actually are, try to avoid them at all costs.

Multiple domains having the same content. In case you are not aware of it, search engines look at domains IP's, registry dates and many others. Having multiple domains having the same exact content is not something you can hide from them. The same goes with content multiplied many times on separate pages, sub domains and forwarding multiple domains to the same content.

Many of the above techniques apply to most search engines and is not entirely for Google only. By having a mind set that you are building your Adsense together with your pages for the human users and not for bots, you can be assured of the great things for your ads and sites.

Not to mention avoiding the wrath of the search engines and getting your Adsense and site account terminated altogether.

www.ingramcontent.com/pod-product-compliance
Lightning Source LLC
Chambersburg PA
CBHW071201220526
45468CB00003B/1109